ON BEING RIGHT

Greenberg's African Linguistic Classification
and the Methodological Principles which Underlie it

by

Paul Newman

Institute for the Study of Nigerian Languages and Cultures
African Studies Program
Indiana University
Bloomington, Indiana
1995

ON BEING RIGHT

Greenberg's African Linguistic Classification
And The Methodological Principles Which Underlie It

When Greenberg's comprehensive African language classification appeared some thirty-five years ago (Greenberg 1955b, 1963), it was greeted with everything from adulation to highly emotional rejection. The negative voices were particular concerned about perceived errors in fact and presumed flaws in methodology, especially relating to the adequacy of the proof. Over time, as the substance of Greenberg's overall classification held up under the careful scrutiny and analysis of other scholars, it gained general acceptance and the methodological discussions died away.

With the publication of Greenberg's *Language in the Americas* (1987), both proponents and opponents of his controversial American Indian classification have taken it upon themselves to make statements of questionable accuracy about his earlier African work. It thus strikes me as essential to address some of the misrepresentations and misunderstandings that have been bandied about. The aim of this paper, then, is to set the record straight with regard to the scholarly importance of Greenberg's African classification and the essence of the methodology that he employed.

Before turning to methodology per se, it is necessary to make it clear that Greenberg's African classification was an accomplishment of major proportions. He set up a broad classificatory scheme which, with subsequent modifications and improvements, has become the standard frame of reference for the entire field of African studies throughout the world. One would hardly need to emphasize the significance of the African language classification were it not for the revisionist history being promulgated by various scholars who have attempted to belittle Greenberg's earlier work. Campbell (1988: 592), e.g., has suggested that the African classification was not an extraordinary feat since (a) the languages are "simply more demonstrably related than American languages are..." and (b) "received opinion concerning African classification at the time was particularly bad." Neither argument is valid. Some African languages, such as a good many Bantu languages, are indeed clearly similar on the surface and, as a result, their relationship has long been recognized. But is this any different from what holds among the languages of the Iroquoian group? Once one moves to relationships that are even slightly more distant, however, the surface resemblances quickly fade away. For example, Yoruba, a Kwa language, does not look at all like Kikongo, a typical Bantu language, although both belong to the same Niger-Congo family. Nor does Margi look like Hausa (both Chadic languages), which is why the late Johannes Lukas (1936), an eminently capable scholar who was a specialist in the languages of the area, originally failed to put them in the same family. Campbell's correct statement that "portions of Greenberg's African classification...are still in dispute" contradicts his earlier assertion that the resemblances are obvious! If responsible linguists disagree as to whether Mande belongs in Niger-Congo, if Songhai belongs in Nilo-Saharan, or if Hadza belongs in Khoisan, it is because the linguistic differences are very great and the relationships not obvious in the least. One has to recognize, moreover, that notions such as "demonstrably related" and "obviously similar" are subjective and vary from person to person and from time to time. What is obviously similar once a relationship has been pointed out and accepted may not have been so obvious beforehand. It is a

2

commonplace in science that empirical clues of all types become easy to see once somebody has finally discovered the solution to a problem. The idea that African classification prior to Greenberg was in a bad state is also incorrect from a historical perspective. With hindsight, we can now say that the prevailing classification was faulty, but there was no sense at the time that anything was seriously wrong. This was not a situation of the type elaborated on by Kuhn (1970) of a field being in a state of anomie because of intellectual crises and contradictions and thus being ripe for a scientific revolution. On the contrary. What Greenberg had to overcome was a received classification about which there was very little controversy or disagreement. The standard classification being adhered to when Greenberg appeared on the scene was that of Meinhof, a scholar of great breadth and knowledge, who was the dominant African linguist of his day. This classification, which organized the languages of the continent into five families (or phyla), namely Semitic, Hamitic, Sudanic, Bantu, and Bushman, had been in place since early in the century (Meinhof 1912; 1915 (popularized by Werner 1925)). It had been adopted wholeheartedly not only by most linguists and anthropologists—Sapir (1913) and certain French scholars (e.g. Meillet and Cohen 1924) being exceptions—but also as a basis for cataloguing by major research libraries around the world (e.g., Hamburg University, University of London, and Columbia University). It is easy after the fact to see that Meinhof's Hamitic family, for example, was based on "now discredited racial principles"; but the fall of the Hamitic myth—if one can speak in such terms of a concept which still lurks in the halls of academe (not to mention the world of semi-science)—was primarily due to Greenberg's linguistic work rather than being a precondition to it. (For a discussion of the Hamitic question see Drake 1959 and Sanders 1969.) Moreover, it is precisely because the Hamitic concept had what was thought to be a solid anthropological/racial basis (cf.

Seligman 1966)—not to mention Biblical credentials—that the validity of Hamitic as a language family seemed reasonable and beyond challenge. Or take the question of Bantu, a large, well-known group of languages stretching across extensive areas of the African continent from Cameroon in the northwest to Kenya in the east to South Africa in the south, whose status as a distinct family has long been recognized—as early, if not even earlier, than Indo-European (Cole 1971). Greenberg's remarkable achievement here was not simply in connecting Bantu to the languages of West Africa— Westermann (1927) had already observed shared features between the two groups that might suggest such a relationship—but in attaching Bantu to a very low node on the tree as a minor subgroup of a group of a branch of the Niger-Congo family. If Greenberg had treated Bantu and the West African "Sudanic" languages as coordinate members of a "Bantu-Sudanic" superfamily, his proposal probably would not have been received with such shock, not to mention hostility; but contrary to the then-accepted viewpoint, which at the time no one saw reason to question, Greenberg insightfully perceived that Bantu was a group of a much lower phylogenetic status. (In what must be regarded as a bit of hyperbole concerning the internal make-up of Bantu and the nearby languages then known as "Semi-Bantu", Greenberg wrote: "The denial of the relationship between the Bantu and Semi-Bantu languages, which is almost comparable to deny[ing] the genetic relationship of British and American English, is the *reductio ad absurdum* of the conventional assumption of the independent status of Bantu" (Greenberg 1955b: 35–36). In the 1963 edition of his work (p. 33), Greenberg repeated the above sentence verbatim but replaced "British and American English" by "English and German".)

When one considers that in the late 1940s Greenberg was a young, unknown American and that African linguistics as represented in the prevailing classifications and university teaching programs was dominated by German and British scholars, one has to acknowledge that Greenberg's comprehensive reclassification of the languages of African was a bold endeavor. In many ways, it was a more difficult task and more of an achievement than his recent American Indian work!

Let us now turn to the question of linguistic methodology and see what a close analysis of Greenberg's African work can tell us about his approach to classification. The best way to analyze Greenberg's method of classification is to forget about methodology in the strict sense of the term and to focus on the historical linguistic principles underlying his work. Much of the misunderstanding (and general pointlessness) of the methodological exchanges between Greenberg and his critics has been due to a failure to appreciate this point. I would argue that Greenberg's success in the African area was due not to the development of new techniques (*pace* Vansina 1979-80), but rather to the elaboration of an insightful and productive scientific viewpoint. Let me illustrate what I mean.

1. LUMPERS VERSUS SPLITTERS

American Indianists who contrast their conservative approach to the "reductionist zeal" of scholars such as Kroeber and Dixon or Sapir (Campbell and Mithun 1979a: 26) invariably place Greenberg in this "lumping tradition". He was also viewed in this light by the "splitters" of the School of Oriental and African Studies, who were extremely hostile to his African work. It is also generally assumed that there is some necessary connection between Greenberg's "loose" method of mass comparison and his predilection for higher level linguistic groupings. A close look at Greenberg's original African work thus turns up some surprising findings.

Greenberg's African classification that is now accepted as the basic framework in the field was presented in 1963 in his book *The Languages of Africa* (Greenberg 1963). In the book, Greenberg "lumped" all the languages of the continent into four phyla:

5

Afroasiatic, Niger-Kordofanian, Nilo-Saharan, and Khoisan. This work, however, was a revision of an earlier classification, which appeared as a series of articles in 1949/1950/1954 and reprinted as a book, *Studies in African Linguistic Classification* (henceforth *SALC*), published in 1955. (In this paper, my references are all to the pagination in the book rather than in the individual articles.) In *SALC*, Greenberg assigned the languages of Africa, which Meinhof had classified into five large families, into sixteen distinct groups. (Ruhlen's statement (1993: 1499) that pror to Greenberg's classification "the over 1,000 African languages had been grouped into dozens of small families, the relationships among which were unknown..." is a gross misrepresentation of the then existing scholarly situation.) Greenberg did combine Bantu with the languages of West Africa, but he took apart Meinhof's broad Sudanic family. Similarly, although he combined Semitic with Ancient Egyptian, Berber, Cushitic, and Chadic into a larger group, he totally dismantled Meinhof's Hamitic family. In other words, while Greenberg's analysis did involve some classification into higher groups, his overall results demonstrate clearly that there was no philosophical or methodological imperative to do so. Greenberg's attitude about his "splitting", which he addressed explicitly, is instructive and deserves to be quoted in full (Greenberg 1955b: 100–101):

> Some may consider the relatively large number of families, compared to previous analyses, an unwelcome result of the present investigation. The number is moderate when contrasted with the American Indian situation, or even that of Eurasia. That there should be sixteen language families in Africa is, I should think, not really surprising in view of the admitted antiquity of Africa as a place of human habitation. Previous investigations have shied away from admitting the

existence of language families of small membership. No doubt large and equally balanced areas on a map and vast syntheses which include languages whose relationship cannot be demonstrated have a certain esthetic appeal, but I do not see that such considerations can play a part in scientific analysis. The results arrived at here for Africa are quite similar to those for North and South America and for Oceania in this respect, that vast areas are occupied by a small number of widely extended families while in other regions numbers of small isolated groups are found. The present results therefore tend to make Africa, in this respect, much more like other areas of the world than has previously appeared to be the case.

As is well-known, Greenberg later assigned the Kordofanian languages to Niger-Congo to form Niger-Kordofanian and he combined the rest of his smaller groups and isolated languages into a new Nilo-Saharan phylum, an extensive and varied group whose genetic unity is reasonably well supported by the evidence, notwithstanding problems and uncertainties at the edges. Whether Greenberg is correct, i.e., whether there are in fact only four phyla for all of Africa, remains to be determined; but the classification is clearly based on a judicious evaluation of extant empirical materials and not on a priori reductionist principles. In terms of his intellectual disposition, there is no question in my mind but that Greenberg has to be placed in the "lumping" tradition. This, however, is not due to any peculiar penchant for large-sized groups or small numbers of groups. Rather, it follows naturally from the goal shared by all scientific comparativists and classifiers, namely to probe the limits of one's field in order to discover valid, albeit previously unrecognized, connections and relationships of a distant nature.

In discussing lumping vs. splitting traditions, there is an often

7

overlooked point that needs to be made. Scholars in the splitting tradition normally characterize themselves and their approach as being "conservative", as contrasted with the wild, profligate approach of the reductionist lumpers. Campbell and Mithun (1979a: 37), in whose book some 62 independent language groups are set up for North America alone, state: "The general attitude reflected in this volume is more conservative than any since Powell." The authors' classification may or may not be the correct one—I leave this to experts in the field to judge—but, the assumption that failing to classify or adopting the weakest classification is in and of itself scientifically conservative and responsible cannot be accepted. From a general scientific perspective this is a blatant error. It is a commonly made error among linguists, but it is an error just the same. Whether a classification is or is not conservative depends on the fit between the classification being proposed and the available facts under consideration, not on the number of groups per se, whether that happens to be large or small. For example, in an extensive inventory of African languages, Mann and Dalby (1987), who present themselves as arch conservatives on matters of African linguistic classification, deny the existence of Chadic as a family (one of Greenberg's five branches within Afroasiatic) and treat seven units that most Chadic specialists, including myself, have analyzed as subgroups within Chadic as independent linguistic groups coordinate with Semitic. Of course they *could* be right that there is no such family as Chadic (although all of the available evidence suggests otherwise), but one has to recognize that *theirs* is the radical proposal. Given the considerable comparative work that has been done on Chadic over the past twenty-five years involving solid morphological as well as lexical reconstructions (cf. Newman 1977), the claim that the 140 or so Chadic languages can be grouped into a single family is the true conservative position whereas the supposed "agnostic/conservative" approach, which treats the unity of Chadic as unproved, is really the radical stance.

8

Critics of Greenberg's African classification have hammered away at the inadequacy of his method of mass comparison for proving the validity of his putative genetic groups. This concern with proof has also characterized the more recent work of American Indianists as indicated by the following quotations: "At the outset, I should indicate that, by the criteria of regular sound correspondences among languages and of the reconstruction of total proto-forms of words, Penutian in the sense used here is not a *proven* genetic relationship" (Silverstein 1979: 650, emphasis mine]). "In fact it is virtually impossible to *prove* distant genetic relationship on the basis of lexical comparisons alone" (Goddard 1975: 254–55, emphasis mine).

There are two significant errors regarding this matter of proof, one specific to Greenberg's methodology and one concerning scientific methodology in general. With regard to Greenberg's approach, it is clear from his writings and discussions that he never conceived of mass comparison as a technique for providing *proof*. As early as 1949, before mass comparison as such had been articulated, Greenberg wrote: "I have given first place in setting up *hypotheses* of relationship to comparisons of vocabulary. I have then followed up such hypotheses with an examination of all available grammatical material" (Greenberg 1955b: 2, emphasis mine). Later, he explicitly described mass comparison as "a method for discovering valid relationships" (Greenberg 1957: 40). In other words, mass comparison for Greenberg was a "discovery procedure", especially intended to probe remote relationships; it was never meant to be a formal method for providing proof.

There is an even more important matter regarding proof that Greenberg has not addressed in the manner it deserves and which I would like to raise here, namely what is it that has to be proved and who has to prove it? Critics of proposed distant relationships have generally demanded that the burden of proof belongs to the person proposing the higher level groups. Thus the argument of the few linguists who still do not accept the membership of Chadic within Afroasiatic is that the relationship has still not been proven conclusively by the evidence (see Cohen 1984, Newman 1980). The unstated assumption has been that the rules of criminal procedure whereby an accused is innocent until proven guilty should be carried over into historical linguistics in the form of a requirement that languages be presumed to be unrelated unless proven otherwise. But is there any justification for this requirement in linguistics (or any other science for that matter)? The misunderstanding constantly arises because the question invariably is wrongly put. If two languages A and B show certain lexical and/or grammatical similarities, the question is not "can one prove that A and B are related?" but rather, "given the observed similarities between the pair of languages (or group of languages), which hypothesis is more reasonable, that A is related to B or that A is not related to B?" Greenberg was within one word of grasping this essential procedural point when he wrote at the very beginning of his African language study: "There is nothing recondite about the methods which I have employed. It is the common-sense recognition that certain resemblances between languages can *only* be explained on the hypothesis of genetic relationship" (Greenberg 1955b: 1). If one replaces the word "only" by "best", so that the phrase reads "... that certain resemblances between languages can *best* be explained on the hypothesis of genetic relationship" it becomes clear that what is at issue is not proof but rather the evaluation of competing hypotheses. Notice that this approach also carries over to many other areas involved in interpreting the evidence on which a proposed classification rests. For example, linguists who reject proposed relationships based on lexical comparisons often charge that the evi*ᵈ* ᵉe is unconvincing since the observed similarities could be due *ⁱ*ng. Of course they could be. But the question is not whether the proponent of the classification can prove conclusively that the resemblances are due to genetic relationship. Rather, given all that we know about borrowing (including phonological replacements, morphological constraints, semantic patterning, susceptibility of basic vs. non-basic words, etc.) and given the historical and geographical situation in which the languages are (or likely were) found, what is the more likely explanation, that the resemblances are due to common origin or to borrowing?

3. THE COMPARATIVE METHOD

There is probably nothing in Greenberg's methodology of classification for which he has been criticized so extensively as his lack of concern for regular sound correspondences and his failure to use the "Comparative Method" (Fodor 1966, Guthrie 1964, Winston 1966). Since Greenberg has dealt with this issue at length in the first chapter of *Language in the Americas*, and since much of the criticism is based on a misunderstanding of the rules of scientific proof, just discussed, I shall not dwell on this matter. By now, people should know that the Comparative Method is a technique for reconstructing aspects of a proto-language by the systematic comparison of languages *already* understood to be related. (Note, for example, Hoenigswald's (1960: 119) definition of the Comparative Method as a "procedure whereby morphs of two or more sister [i.e. genetically related] languages are matched in order to reconstruct the ancestor language.") It has never been an essential tool in the establishment of relationship as such, although it has often been helpful in sorting out problems of subgrouping.

I would, however, like to make one brief observation regarding sound correspondences and distant relationships. Whatever value the establishment of regular sound correspondences might or might not have in determining the nature of linguistic groups and families, it is hopeless to see in this a tool for exploring more remote

11

relationships, which is why "adventurous" scholars such as Sapir and Swadesh have not felt constrained by it (Swadesh 1954, Voegelin 1942). Campbell and Mithun (1979a: 47) make the following remarkable statement: "The methods for *establishing* distant genetic relationships have not been very different from the method used at the family level, namely the comparative method." If this statement is taken as a description of what scholars have done in the past, then it is clearly false. Whatever procedures were employed in establishing the now generally accepted families such as Indo-European, Afroasiatic, Niger-Congo, or Uralic, it was not by the systematic use of the comparative method. If Campbell and Mithun's statement is taken as a guide as to how one *ought* to proceed in the case of possible distant relationships, then I would contend that it is misguided and defeatist. The fact that these authors were forced to postulate 62 distinct families for North America alone shows in unmistakable terms that their method cannot produce results once one leaves the realm of the closely and obviously related. As anyone who has ever attempted to establish regular correspondences knows, it is not an easy task even when one is dealing with a moderately shallow time depth (let's say 5,000 years). When the time depth is double or triple that amount, lexical loss, semantic change, and the effects of morphologically conditioned changes and phonological erosion so distort the evidence that it is almost impossible to establish recurrent and regular phonological correspondences. *To insist that relationships can only be established by the comparative method is to reject in advance the possibility that remote relationships that we presume must exist can ever be discovered.* I am not sure how one does go about establishing remote genetic relationships—and Greenberg's approach obviously leaves much to be desired—but it is most certainly *not* by limiting oneself to phenomena and methods which are only applicable, if at all, to closely related languages. As we know from the experience of other sciences, sound, well-established methods that apply to normal things in our everyday world do not necessarily work when one studies things that are extremely small or extremely fast or extremely distant. Greenberg's approach to remote language classification may prove to be unworkable and unreliable; but if so the task for the next generation of linguists has to be to find a better alternative. Limiting oneself in advance to a rigid "Neo-Newtonian historical/comparative linguistics" is definitely not the answer.

4. VOCABULARY VS. MORPHOLOGY

Scholars have long debated the question whether the criteria for genetic classification should be primarily lexical or morphological/grammatical (see Lackner and Rowe 1955). The following statement by Bergsland (1951: 168) is typical of the grammaticalist position: "Problems of historical relationship should, if possible, be discussed first in terms of the grammatical elements which make up the basic structural features of the languages compared." Writing much earlier, Meillet and Cohen (1924: 6–7) argue for the stability of grammar over vocabulary, and thus its value for historical classification, in even stronger terms: "La part de la langue qui se maintient de génération en génération en se transformant progressivement est le système grammatical.... En revanche, le vocabulaire est sujet à des innovations brusques et capricieuses." ["The part of language which lasts from generation to generation, gradually being transformed in the process is the grammatical system.... Vocabulary, on the other hand, is subject to abrupt and capricious innovations."] Greenberg has generally been regarded as belonging to the lexicalist camp and has commonly been criticized for his overdependence on lexical evidence to the exclusion of other types of evidence (Campbell 1988, esp. pp. 595–96). However, a close look at Greenberg's African work, together with his overt methodological statements, allows one to develop a more accurate picture of where Greenberg really stands on this question.

The fact is that Greenberg has always accorded importance to grammatical materials in his classificatory work and has used them and cited them extensively. In presenting his four major African language families, Greenberg devoted most of the discussion to detailed grammatical comparisons. Each discussion was accompanied by a comparative word list to be sure, but the grammatical evidence was given at least as much prominence as the lexical evidence, if not more. The grouping of Bantu into Niger-Congo, for example, possibly could have been done on lexical materials alone, but Greenberg's treatment of functioning and vestigial noun class systems in the languages of West Africa suggests what the key criterion was. In the case of the relationship established later between Niger-Congo and the Kordofanian languages, noun class systems played an even more important role. With regard to the incorporation of Chadic into an all-embracing Afroasiatic phylum, the evidence provided in the initial classification was primarily grammatical, as was the important evidence published later in key articles (Greenberg 1952, 1955a, 1960). It is interesting to note that one reviewer of *Language in the Americas* who was very critical of the lexical comparisons found the grammatical evidence for the Amerind phylum to be impressive (Liedtke 1989: 284): "Dieser Teil seiner Arbeit ist brilliant und von unschätzbaren Wert für seine Beweisführung." ["This part of his work is brilliant and of inestimable value for his claim."]

In considering the use of grammatical evidence for classification, Greenberg was particularly impressed with the probative value of suppletion: "Even one instance of this...virtually guarantees genetic relationship" (Greenberg 1953: 271). In comparing other grammatical elements, there was a play-off between their disadvantage in generally being phonologically short and their advantage in being relatively resistant to borrowing and other external influences. "The oft repeated maxim of the superiority of grammatical over vocabulary evidence for relationship owes what validity it has to this relative impermeability of derivational and inflectional morphemes to borrowing" (Greenberg 1953: 274).

The essential point as far as Greenberg is concerned is that there is no conflict between relationships based on lexical as opposed to grammatical evidence. As discussed earlier, Greenberg's operational procedure in the African classification was to use lexical comparison as a discovery tool: "I have given first place in setting up hypotheses of relationship to comparisons of vocabulary" (Greenberg 1955b: 2). But note the continuation of his methodological statement: "I have then followed up such hypotheses with an examination of all available grammatical material. In not a single instance have I been forced to retract an initial thesis which seemed probable on the basis of lexical resemblances." I suspect that the situation is not quite as simple and straightforward as Greenberg makes it sound, but the general matching of results regardless of the kind of comparative materials used shouldn't be surprising. As Weinreich (1958: 377) has noted, "In the well-known comparative fields, basic vocabulary and basic grammar have always been found to develop together."

So, where has the idea come from that Greenberg had reservations about the use of grammatical materials for genetic classification? At the very beginning of his African study, Greenberg wrote: "But under no circumstances can we reject results attained from obvious lexical resemblances in fundamental vocabulary in favor of those based on vague structural traits" (Greenberg 1955b: 2). The key word here is "vague". As shown clearly in his own work, Greenberg placed a high value on *specific* grammatical correspondences that displayed similarities in form as well as in meaning and structure. What Greenberg was objecting to was the use—clearly "misuse" is more appropriate—of vague *typological* similarities for historical/genetic classification. Typologically induced errors in previous African classifications had occurred in two directions. Unwarranted higher-level groups had been set up primarily on the basis of shared typological features, e.g. the lumping of disparate languages into Hamitic primarily because they happened to have grammatical gender. Conversely, valid genetic groups had been overlooked because of the absence of supposedly diagnostic features, e.g. the classification of Chadic languages into two distinct families because of the presence or absence of gender, or the exclusion of various languages from Bantu because they did not have a vowel system with a balanced odd number of vowels (preferably seven, but five or nine would do). Greenberg (in Bateman et al. 1990: 19) has recently commented, and in this case I think that he is reliable as a self historian: "It was the elimination of typological criteria that was the single most important factor in the success of my African classification." The distinction between lexical and grammatical evidence, on the other hand, was not a significant one in principle. In practice, lexical comparisons might be preferred over grammatical comparisons because of problems of limited choice and convergence affecting the latter, but the distinction was not fundamental. What was fundamental was the idea that no matter what kind of materials one used, a historical/genetic classification should clearly be that, and not a racial or typological or areal classification!

5. MASS COMPARISON

If there is one technique with which Greenberg's name is most closely associated, it is the method of mass comparison (or "multilateral comparison" as he now prefers to call it). Ironically, given the attention that mass comparison /as received over the years, this so-called method hardly qualifies to be characterized as such. Although Greenberg's methodological statements, replete with mathematical calculations, give the impression that mass comparison is a precise technique, which presumably could be employed by other scholars, there is little evidence that he himself ever used it in such a way. Anyone reading chapter 1, the methodological chapter, of Greenberg's *The Languages of Africa* (1963) would be led to believe that Greenberg was describing the technique that he had used in coming up with the classification presented in the rest of the book. A look at the earlier edition of Greenberg's African work shows that such was not the case. In the brief methodological remarks at the beginning of the original study, which first appeared in article form in 1949, there was no mention of mass comparison. The term does not appear until 1954 when Greenberg published an article (included as the *last* chapter of *SALC*) as a response to the methodological attacks of his critics. In other words, mass comparison was a method invented after the fact. Greenberg even acknowledged as much with specific reference to the probabilistic evidentiary power of mass comparison: "In fact, I had no such considerations in mind when I first undertook the present classification" (Greenberg 1955b: 107).

In methodological discussions, Greenberg has often repeated the claim that mass comparison's effectiveness in identifying true cognates (and thus in relating languages) derives from mathematical/probability considerations. As many of Greenberg's critics have pointed out, the problem with mass comparison as generally applied is that it suffers from, rather than benefits from, the chance factor. That is, if one can freely pick and choose examples from a hundred or so languages, one has a hundred times as many chances of finding random look-alikes than if one is systematically comparing a pair or a small group of languages. When one adds to this the fact that one *must* allow for semantic shift, then the number of possible look-alikes for each comparison must be multiplied five-fold again. (Let me note that although semantic leeway in equating potential cognates is troubling from a practical point of view because of the lack of clear constraints, one cannot just rule it out by fiat. Taken literally, the assertion by Campbell and Mithun (1979a: 54) that "Proposed cognates should be semantically equivalent," a statement echoing the earlier insistence of Guthrie (1962), is totally absurd. As all historical linguists know, semantic shift is a pervasive and extremely common type of language change, one that is easily observable even in the case of languages as closely related as English and Dutch.)

Although I am critical of mass comparison for what it is not, namely a precise, formal method, I do not want to give the impression that it was unimportant to Greenberg's success in the African area. Viewed as a cover-term for an overall operational approach, multilateral comparison *does* make sense as a means of exploring more distant relationships and Greenberg *did* make use of it in his African classification. Three areas particularly deserve brief discussion.

The first is that genetic relationships in linguistics are transitive. If A is related to B, B is related to C, and C is related to D, then A are D are necessarily related, *even if* these languages synchronically bear no resemblance to one another. This possibility was recognized by Meillet and Cohen (1924: 2) over a half century ago: "Des langues parentes peuvent différer entre elles au point que la parenté ne soit reconnaissable à aucun trait." ["Related languages can differ from one another to the point where the relationship is not recognizable in a single trait."] Languages form chains of relationship and exhibit interlocking pieces of material preserved from the common ancestor. Multilateral comparison allows one to identify chains that could not possibly be assembled by dealing with just a couple of links at a time.

The second point is that establishing relationship per se is really a minor part of linguistic classification. The important task is determining that some specific languages constitute a valid group *as opposed to* some other languages. In a sense, then, all linguistic classification is subclassification. Given that scholars have always employed multi-language comparison in attacking problems of subclassification, it is only natural that linguistic classification in general should take such an approach.

18

The third point has to do with mass comparison as a discovery tool in a cognitive sense. Mass comparison of vocabulary is often thought of as a shallow surface operation, something that a computer, for example, might be able to do. What it really is, however, is an immersion technique. Scholars such as Greenberg look at lots of languages at one time because they thereby develop a "feel"—Voegelin (1942), referring to Sapir, termed it "insight"—for how specific groups of languages work and what kinds of similarities tend to recur. Comparative linguists often think of concepts such as resemblance or similarity as basic givens found in the external world; but in reality they are relative evaluative terms that derive from broad familiarity with a large number and wide array of languages. The method of mass comparison is not quite comparable to classification by Gestalt, but it is not a totally inappropriate way to think of it.

6. CONCLUSION

In conclusion, the success of Greenberg's African classification was not due to the use of a superior methodology in the narrow sense of the term. The correct groupings did not emerge from the strict application of a specific method nor were the errors methodologically induced. Rather, it was the solid foundation provided by Greenberg's overall intellectual scientific stance that helped shield him from the errors of the past and allowed him to look at the evidence in a new light. The three key elements in his approach were: (a) focusing clearly on evidence leading to a historical/genetic classification as opposed to data relating to questions of language typology or language contact; (b) eliminating the misleading "noise" provided by racial and cultural considerations, and (c) developing a broad "wide-angle" perspective by comparing a large number of languages together rather than proceeding pair-wise in a step-by-step fashion. A combination of hard work, imagination, and insight plus a courageous independence of spirit ultimately led to his unequaled achievement in the field of African linguistic classification. In the case of Greenberg's American Indian work, it may be, as his critics contend, that something went wrong in the recording and analysis of primary data leading to unwarranted assertions of specious relationships (although given his remarkable track record in the past, I personally wouldn't jump to such a conclusion); but the discussion needs to focus on substantive issues directly related to the analysis of American Indian languages and not on pseudo-issues of methodology. There is nothing to be gained by trying to undermine the essence of Greenberg's essentially sound classificatory approach nor in trying to rewrite history as far as the significance of his African language classification is concerned.

Acknowledgements: The original version of this paper was presented at "Language and Prehistory in the Americas: A Conference on the Greenberg Classification", organized by Allan Taylor at the University of Colorado, Boulder, March 22–25, 1990. The present text incorporates ideas presented at the First World Congress of African Linguistics, University of Swaziland, July 18–22, 1994. Attendance at the Congress was made possible by travel grants from the National Science Foundation (administered through the Linguistic Society of America), and from the Office of International Programs and the College of Arts and Sciences, Indiana University. I am grateful to Robert Shull for assistance in the design and production of this publication.

BIBLIOGRAPHY

A *CA* book review: Language in the Americas. *Current Anthropology* 28: 647–67 (1987).

Bateman, Richard, et al. 1990. Speaking of forked tongues: the feasibility of reconciling human phylogeny and the history of language. *Current Anthropology* 31: 1–24.

Bendor-Samuel, John (ed.). 1989. *The Niger-Congo Languages.* Lanham, MD: University Press of America.

Bergsland, Knut. 1951. Kleinschmidt centennial IV: Aleut demonstratives, Aleut-Eskimo relationship. *International Journal of American Linguistics* 17: 167–79.

Campbell, Lyle. 1988. Review article on *Language in the Americas* by Joseph H. Greenberg. *Language* 64: 591–615.

Campbell, Lyle, and Marianne Mithun. 1979a. Introduction: North American Indian historical linguistics in current perspective. In *The Languages of Native America: Historical and Comparative Assessment,* ed. by Lyle Campbell and Marianne Mithun, pp. 3–69. Austin: University of Texas Press.

Campbell, Lyle, and Marianne Mithun. 1979b. *The Languages of Native America: Historical and Comparative Assessment.* Austin: University of Texas Press.

Cohen, David. 1984. Review of *The Classification of Chadic within Afroasiatic* by Paul Newman. *Bulletin de la Société de Linguistique de Paris* 79(2): 334–45.

Cole, Desmond T. 1971. The history of African linguistics to 1945. In *Current Trends in Linguistics, Vol. 7: Linguistics in Sub-Saharan Africa,* ed. by Thomas A. Sebeok, pp. 1–29. The Hague: Mouton.

Dalby, David. 1966. Levels of relationship in the comparative study of African languages. *African Language Studies* 7: 171-79.

Der-Houssikian, Haig. 1972. The evidence for a Niger-Congo hypothesis. *Cahiers d'Études Africaines* 12(46): 316–22.

Drake, Saint-Clair. 1959. Détruire le mythe chamitique, devoir des hommes cultivés. *Présence africaine* 24/25: 215–30.

Flight, Colin. 1981. Trees and traps: Strategies for the classification of African languages and their historical significance. *History in Africa* 8: 43-74.

Fodor, István. 1966. *The Problems in the Classification of the African Languages: Methodological and Theoretical Conclusions concerning the Classification System of Joseph H. Greenberg.* (Studies on Developing Countries.) Budapest: Center for Afro-Asian Research of the Hungarian Academy of Sciences. — [Rev. by Joseph H. Greenberg, *Language* 45: 427–32 (1969).]

Goddard, Ives. 1975. Algonquian, Wiyot, and Yurok: proving a distant genetic relationship. In *Linguistics and Anthropology: In Honor of C. F. Voegelin*, ed. by M. Dale Kinkade, Kenneth L. Hale and Oswald Werner, pp. 249–62. Lisse: Peter de Ridder Press.

Goodman, Morris. 1970. Some questions on the classification of African languages. *International Journal of American Linguistics* 36: 117–22.

Greenberg, Joseph H. 1948. The classification of African languages. *American Anthropologist* 50: 24-30.

Greenberg, Joseph H. 1952. The Afro-Asiatic (Hamito-Semitic) present. *Journal of the American Oriental Society* 72: 1–9.

Greenberg, Joseph H. 1953. Historical linguistics and unwritten languages. In *Anthropology Today*, ed. by A. L. Kroeber, pp. 265–86. Chicago: University of Chicago Press.

Greenberg, Joseph H. 1955a. Internal a-plurals in Afroasiatic (Hamito-Semitic). In *Afrikanistische Studien* [Festschrift Westermann], ed. by Johannes Lukas, pp. 198–204. Berlin.

Greenberg, Joseph H. 1955b. *Studies in African Linguistic Classification*. New Haven: The Compass Publishing Company. — [Rev. by J. Berry, *Bulletin of the School of Oriental and African Studies* 18: 395 (1956); Wm. E. Welmers, *Language* 32: 556–57 (1956); H. A. Gleason, *American Anthropologist* 58: 948–49 (1956); A. E. Meeussen, "Hamietisch en Nilotisch" [rev. article], *Zaïre* 11: 263–72 (1957).]

Greenberg, Joseph H. 1957. *Essays in Linguistics.* Chicago: University of Chicago Press.

Greenberg, Joseph H. 1960. An Afro-Asiatic pattern of gender and number agreement. *Journal of the American Oriental Society* 80: 317–21.

Greenberg, Joseph H. 1963. *The Languages of Africa.* Bloomington: Indiana University. (Reprinted with minor corrections, 1966, The Hague: Mouton). — [Rev. by A. E. Meeussen, *Journal of African Languages* 2: 170–71 (1963);Wm. E. Welmers, *Word* 19: 407–17 (1963); M. Guthrie, *Journal of African History* 5: 135–36 (1964); M. Houis, *Bulletin de l'Institut Fondamental d'Afrique Noire* 26: 286–95 (1964); B. Siertsema, *Forum des Letteren* 5: 103–104 (1964); B. Siertsema, *Lingua* 13: 85–87 (1964); E. Westphal, *American Anthropologist* 66: 1446–49 (1964); J. Delord, *La Linguistique* 1: 142–44 (1965); V. Monteil, "La classification des langues de l'Afrique" [rev. article], *Bulletin de l'Institut Fondamental d'Afrique Noire* 27: 155–68 (1965); P. F. Lacroix, *Bulletin de la Société de Linguistique de Paris* 61(2): 208–14 (1966).]

Greenberg, Joseph H. 1987. *Language in the Americas.* Stanford: Stanford University Press.

Greenberg, Joseph H. 1989. Classification of American Indian languages: A reply to Campbell. *Language* 65: 107–14.

Guthrie, Malcolm. 1962. A two-stage method of comparative Bantu study. *African Language Studies* 3: 1–24

Guthrie, Malcolm. 1964. Review of *The Languages of Africa* by Joseph H. Greenberg. *Journal of African History* 5:135–36.

Hoenigswald, Henry M. 1960. *Language Change and Linguistic Reconstruction.* Chicago: University of Chicago Press.

Kuhn, Thomas S. 1970. *The Structure of Scientific Revolutions*, 2nd ed. Chicago: University of Chicago Press.

Lackner, Jerome A., and John H. Rowe. 1955. Morphological similarity as a criterion of genetic relationship between languages. *American Anthropologist* 57: 126–29.

Liedtke, Stefan. 1989. Review of *Language in the Americas* by Joseph H. Greenberg. *Anthropos* 84: 283–85.

Lukas, Johannes. 1936. The linguistic situation in the Lake Chad area in central Africa. *Africa* 9: 332–49.

Mann, Michael, and David Dalby. 1987. *A Thesaurus of African Languages. A Classified and Annotated Inventory of the Spoken Languages of Africa. With an Appendix on their Written Representation.* London: Hans Zell Publishers. — [Rev. by Paul Newman, *Journal of African Languages and Linguistics* 11: 175–82 (1989).]

Meillet, Antoine, and Marcel Cohen. 1924. *Les langues du monde.* Paris: Champion.

Meinhof, Carl. 1912. *Die Sprachen der Hamiten.* Hamburg: L. Friederichsen.

Meinhof, Carl. 1915. *An Introduction to the Study of African Languages.* London: J. M. Dent & Sons.

Newman, Paul. 1970. Historical sound laws in Hausa and in Dera (Kanakuru). *Journal of West African Languages* 7: 39–51.

Newman, Paul. 1977. Chadic classification and reconstructions. *Afroasiatic Linguistics* 5: 1–42.

Newman, Paul. 1980. *The Classification of Chadic within Afroasiatic.* Leiden: Universitaire Pers.

Newman, Paul. 1993. Greenberg's American Indian classification: A report on the controversy. In *Historical Linguistics 1991: Papers from the 10th International Conference on Historical Linguistics*, ed. by Jaap van Marle, pp. 229–42. Amsterdam: Benjamins.

Nicolaï, Robert. 1990. *Parentés linguistiques (à propos du songhay).* Paris: CNRS. — [Rev. by Gerrit Dimmendaal, *Bulletin of the School of Oriental and African Studies* 55: 610-12 (1992).]

Ruhlen, Merritt. 1987. *A Guide to the World's Languages. Volume 1: Classification.* Stanford: Stanford University Press.

Ruhlen, Merritt. 1993. Greenberg, Joseph H. (1915-). In *The Encyclopedia of Language and Linguistics*, pp. 1499-1500. Oxford: Pergamon Press.

24

Sanders, Edith R. 1969. The Hamitic hypothesis: its origin and function in time perspective. *Journal of African History* 10: 521–32.

Sapir, Edward. 1913. Review of *Die Sprachen der Hamiten*, by Carl Meinhof. *Current Anthropological Literature* 2: 21–27.

Sapir, Edward. 1929. Central and North American languages. In *Encyclopaedia Britannica*, pp. 138–41.

Seligman, C. G. 1966. *Races of Africa*. 4th ed. London: Oxford University Press.

Silverstein, Michael. 1979. Penutian: An assessment. In *The Languages of Native America: Historical and Comparative Assessment*, ed. by Lyle Campbell and Marianne Mithun, pp. 650–91. Austin: University of Texas Press.

Swadesh, Morris. 1954. Perspectives and problems of Amerindian comparative linguistics. *Word* 10: 306–32.

Vansina, Jan. 1979-80. Bantu in the crystal ball. *History in Africa* 6: 287-333; 7: 293-325.

Voegelin, Charles F. 1942. Sapir: Insight and rigor. *American Anthropologist* 44: 322–24.

Weinreich, Uriel. 1958. On the compatibility of genetic relationship and convergent development. *Word* 14: 374–79.

Werner, Alice. 1925. *The Language-Families of Africa*. 2nd ed. London: Kegan Paul.

Westermann, Diedrich. 1927. *Die westlichen Sudansprachen und ihre Beziehungen zum Bantu*. (Mitteilungen des Seminars für Orientalische Sprachen, Beiheft, 30.) Berlin.

Westermann, Diedrich. 1935. Charakter und Einteilung der Sudan Sprachen. *Africa* 8: 129-48.

Westermann, Diedrich. 1952. African linguistic classification. *Africa* 22: 250–56.

Winston, F. D. D. 1966. Greenberg's classification of African languages. *African Language Studies* 7: 160–71.